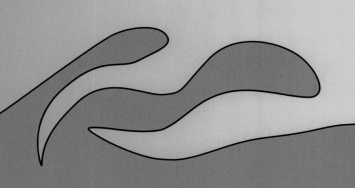

Wild Rides

Wild About

Hot Rods

J. Poolos

PowerKiDS press

New York

Published in 2008 by The Rosen Publishing Group, Inc.
29 East 21st Street, New York, NY 10010

First Edition

Editor: Amelie von Zumbusch
Book Design: Greg Tucker
Photo Researcher: Nicole Pristash

Photo Credits: Cover, pp. 5, 9, 11, 13, 21 Shutterstock.com; p. 7 © Ron Kimball/Ron Kimball Stock; pp. 15, 17 © Getty Images; p. 19 by Kyle Guisewhite.

Library of Congress Cataloging-in-Publication Data

Poolos, Jamie.
    Wild about hot rods / J. Poolos.
        p. cm. — (Wild rides)
    Includes index.
    ISBN-13: 978-1-4042-3790-2 (library binding)
    ISBN-10: 1-4042-3790-9 (library binding)
    1. Hot rods—Juvenile literature. 2. Automobiles—Customizing—United States—Juvenile literature.
I. Title.
    TL236.3.P66 2008
    629.222—dc22
                                                    2006100597

Manufactured in the United States of America

Contents

What Is a Hot Rod?   4

T–Buckets   6

Making a Hot Rod   8

Cool Paint Jobs   10

Hot–Rod Engines   12

The Hot–Rod Age   14

Show Cars   16

Rat Rods   18

Events and Shows   20

Hot Rods Forever!   22

Glossary   23

Index   24

Web Sites   24

What Is a Hot Rod?

A hot rod is an old car that has been changed so that it looks cool and goes fast. Hot rods have powerful **engines** and lightweight bodies. Hot-rod engines are tuned to make the cars go fast. Some hot rod builders cut off the **hood** so people can see and hear the car's big engine.

The lighter a car is, the faster it moves. Therefore, hot-rod owners often make their cars light by removing their heavy parts, such as the roof, hood, **bumpers**, and **fenders**. Owners add colorful paint, fat tires, and **chrome** to make their hot rods look cool.

The builders of this hot rod worked hard to make the car fast, shiny, and colorful.

T-Buckets

Any **coupe** or **roadster** makes a good hot rod. The first hot rods were built from cars that were made by the carmakers Ford and Chevrolet before 1940. One such car is the Ford Model T. The Model T was one of the first cars ever sold.

Hot rods made from Model Ts are called T-buckets. The Model T was perfect for hot rodding because the cars were easy to find in **junkyards**. Hot-rod builders bought the old cars for little money. They used old parts to fix the cars up and turned them into hot rods.

This hot rod is a T-bucket. It was made from a 1923 Ford Model T.

Making a Hot Rod

The first thing hot rod builders do after bringing an old car home is to take off all the parts they do not need. They often use a power saw to cut off the fenders and other body parts, like the roof. Builders sometimes change the shape of the car by making the roof lower or making the fenders stick out.

Once they have finished changing the car's shape, builders add wide back wheels and small front wheels to give it true hot-rod style. For the finishing touches, builders make **custom** headlights and bumpers.

This hot rod's fenders have been taken off. It also has custom headlights and wheels made of chrome.

9

Cool Paint Jobs

What better way to dress up a hot rod than with a cool paint job? Hot-rod owners use many kinds of paint for their cars. Some hot rods are painted in a single, shiny color. Other hot rods have **flat** paint. This makes the car look older.

Some hot rods have metal-flake paint. This paint has tiny pieces of metal inside that make the paint shine. Candy paint is also popular. Candy paint is a very shiny paint in bright colors that look like candy. Many painters add flames or thin lines called pinstripes to make their cars special.

This colorful hot rod has flames painted on it. Many owners paint their hot rods this way.

Hot-Rod Engines

Hot rods each look a little different, but they all have powerful engines. The old cars used to make hot rods were made with small engines. A hot-rod builder takes a bigger, more powerful engine from a newer car and fits it into the **chassis** of one of these old cars. The Chevy small-block V8 and the Ford flathead are the two best-known hot-rod engines.

Since hot-rod engines are often in plain view, many people add chrome to some of the engine parts to make them look good. They also put in cool **exhaust** pipes.

Many hot rod engines are so interesting-looking that owners cut off the cars' hoods to make the engines easier to see.

13

The Hot-Rod Age

The hot rod age began in 1945 and lasted through the 1960s. Young people who wanted fast, cheap cars turned to hot rods. They were proud to build the cars themselves. They enjoyed **drag racing** their cars. They **cruised** the cars and showed them off at places like drive-in movie theaters.

By the 1960s, few of the old junkyard cars people used to make hot rods were left. However, people still wanted fast, cheap cars. Carmakers realized this, so they decided to make inexpensive cars with powerful engines, just like hot rods. These cars are called muscle cars.

This picture from 1955 shows two men working on a hot rod. They are at a drag racing track in Westhampton, New York.

15

Show Cars

Today, hot rods are popular once again. Some of today's hot rods are show cars. Almost every part of a show car is custom built. These hot rods are perfect in every way. They are so expensive that owners will not drive them on the street. Instead, they tow the cars to car shows and hot-rod-club meetings.

There are even television shows about hot-rod building! On these shows, star hot-rod builders, like Boyd Coddington and Jesse James, explain how these fast machines are made. They take part in **contests** to see who can build the coolest hot rod.

Jesse James, seen here, is on a TV show called *Monster Garage.* *On this show, people make hot rods and other wild cars.*

Rat Rods

Some of today's hot rods are made just for driving and racing. These homemade cars are called rat rods. They are made from parts of different kinds of cars. Rat rods have big back wheels and small front wheels. They have dull paint and sit low to the ground. Rat rods are also known as hardcore rods.

Rat-rod owners do not care how their cars look. They just want cars that work well and go fast. Most important, the cars have to be cheap. Rat rods are popular in countries around the world, such as Sweden and Australia.

The rat rod shown here was made from an old truck.

Events and Shows

Hot-rod owners have a lot of fun. They go to club events all over to show their cars. The events are also a good time to talk with other hot-rod owners. Owners drive their hot rods in parades and vote on who has the best hot rod or the coolest paint job.

Owners of expensive show cars take their hot rods to car shows. These hot rods are sometimes called trailer queens because their owners pull them on **trailers**. Hot-rod shows are a great place to see the brightest and most beautiful hot rods.

This hot rod is being shown at a car show. The hood is up so that people can see its shiny engine.

Hot Rods Forever!

When it comes to cars, hot-rod owners believe that if you want something done right, you have to do it yourself. They take great pride in making special, one-of-a-kind cars out of parts found in a junkyard. It is this inventive spirit that keeps the hot-rod world going.

Hot rods just might be the coolest cars on the road. They are light and fast, and they look great. Whether you prefer a fast rat rod or a show car that is a work of art, there is a hot rod for everyone!

Glossary

bumpers (BUM-purz) Bars at the front and back of a car that keep the car safe.

chassis (CHA-see) The part that holds up the body of a car.

chrome (KROHM) A shiny metal that is used on cars and motorcycles.

contests (KAN-tests) Games in which two or more people try to win a prize.

coupe (KOOP) A kind of car with two doors and a hard roof.

cruised (KROOZD) Drove a car slowly to show it off.

custom (KUS-tum) Made in a certain way for a person.

drag racing (DRAG RAY-sing) A kind of racing in which two cars try to pick up the most speed on a short track.

engines (EN-jinz) Machines inside cars or airplanes that make the cars or airplanes move.

exhaust (ig-ZOST) Smoky air made by using gas, oil, or coal.

fenders (FEN-durz) Guards that go over the wheels of a car.

flat (FLAT) Dull, not shiny.

hood (HUD) The cover over a car's engine.

junkyards (JUNGK-yarhdz) Places where trash has been thrown away.

roadster (ROHD-ster) An open car with one big seat in the front.

trailers (TRAY-lerz) Large things with wheels that are pulled by a car or a truck.

Index

A
Australia, 18

B
bumpers, 4, 8

C
chassis, 12
chrome, 4, 12
contests, 16

E
exhaust pipes, 12

F
fenders, 4, 8

flames, 10,
Ford Model T, 6

H
headlights, 8
hood, 4

J
James, Jesse, 16,
junkyard(s), 6, 14, 22

M
muscle cars, 14

P
pinstripes, 10

power saw, 8

R
roadster, 6
roof, 4, 8

S
Sweden, 18

T
tires, 4,
trailer(s), 20,

W
wheels, 8, 18

Web Sites

Due to the changing nature of Internet links, PowerKids Press has developed an online list of Web sites related to the subject of this book. This site is updated regularly. Please use this link to access the list:
www.powerkidslinks.com/wild/hot/